Conten

Age-Appropriate Skills

Language

- following directions
- story comprehension
- descriptive and comparative language
- categorization
- letter recognition and phonemic awareness
- statements and questions
- auditory and visual discrimination
- left-to-right tracking
- oral language
- vocabulary and concept development
- sequencing
- color words

Math

- counting to 20
- patterning
- numeral recognition
- geometric shapes
- ordinal numbers
- beginning computation
- one-to-one matching

Dear Parent,

The stories in this book have themes related to weather conditions, daily weather changes, and how weather helps us. Use the stories to introduce vocabulary and concepts related to weather.

Reading stories aloud will help your child develop a love of reading, and it has proven to enhance a variety of early language skills, including:

- letter recognition and phonemic awareness,
- auditory and visual discrimination,
- left-to-right tracking, and
- vocabulary and concept development.

As you read to your child, remember to:

- speak clearly and with interest.
- track words by moving your finger under each word as you read it.
- ask your child to identify objects in the pictures. Talk about these objects together.
- allow your child to express his or her own thoughts and ideas and to ask you questions.

Support and guide your child as he or she completes the activities. Recognize the efforts your child has made and encourage your child as he or she learns to master basic skills.

We hope your child enjoys these stories and activities.

Sincerely,
Evan-Moor Educational Publishers

Wondering About the Weather

What will the weather be like today?
Will I stay in or go outside to play?

Will it be windy?

Will it be sunny?

3

4

Will it be rainy?

Will it be stormy?

Or will it snow?

The only way to know is to look out the window. Wow! A rainbow!

8

The End

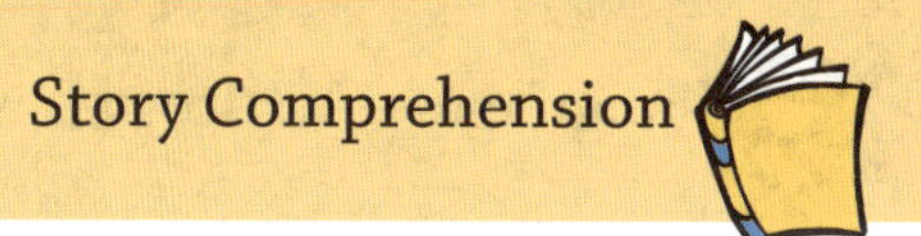

Dressing for the Weather

Draw a line to match.

Note: Children color the pictures that begin with the same sound as the first picture in each row.

Weather Words

Look at the first picture in each row.

Color the pictures that begin with the same sound.

Note: Children count the items in each box and write the number on the line. Children then color the circle in the side of the box that has more items.

Which Has More?

Count. Write. Color.

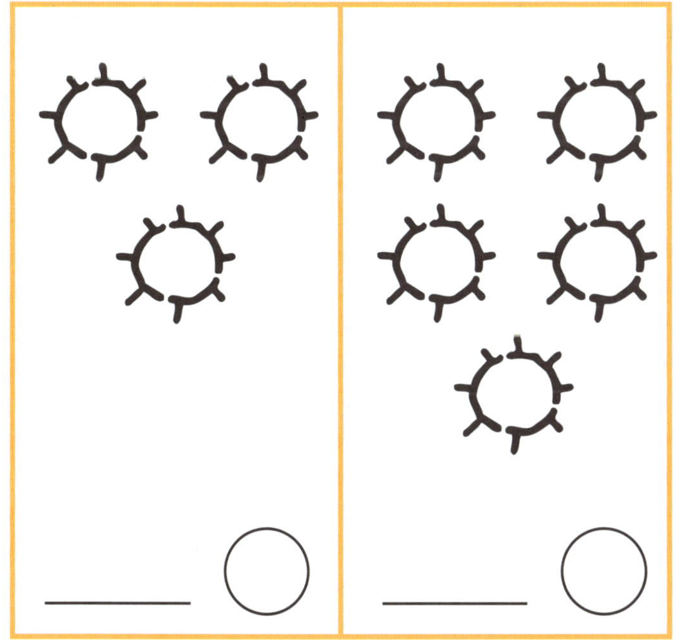

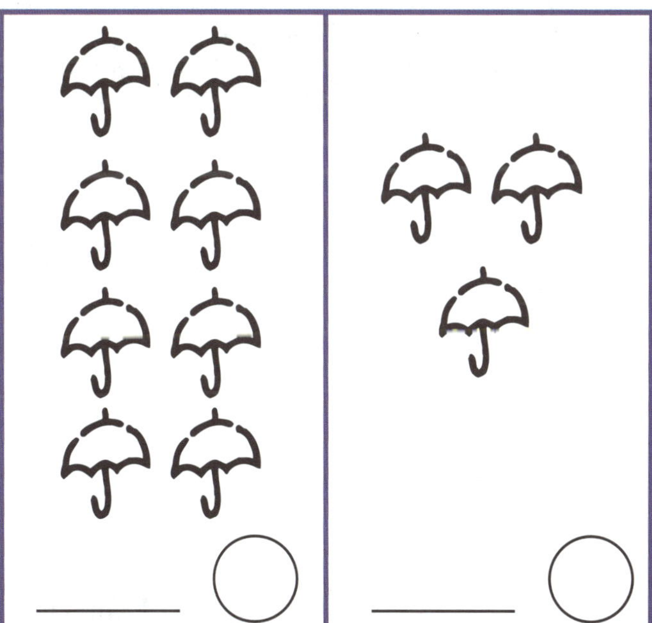

Note: Review color words with children. You may wish to display a chart with the colors and their names as a guide for young learners.

Count the Overalls

Color the 2nd pair of overalls  green.

Color the 5th pair of overalls 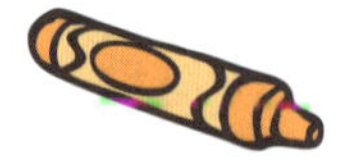 orange.

Color the 3rd pair of overalls 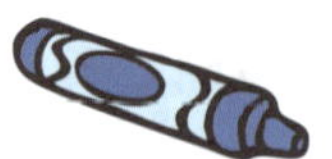 blue.

Color the 1st pair of overalls 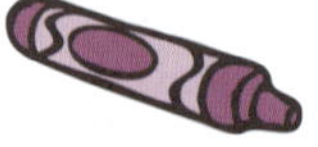 purple.

Color the 4th pair of overalls  red.

A Wonderful Week
of Weather

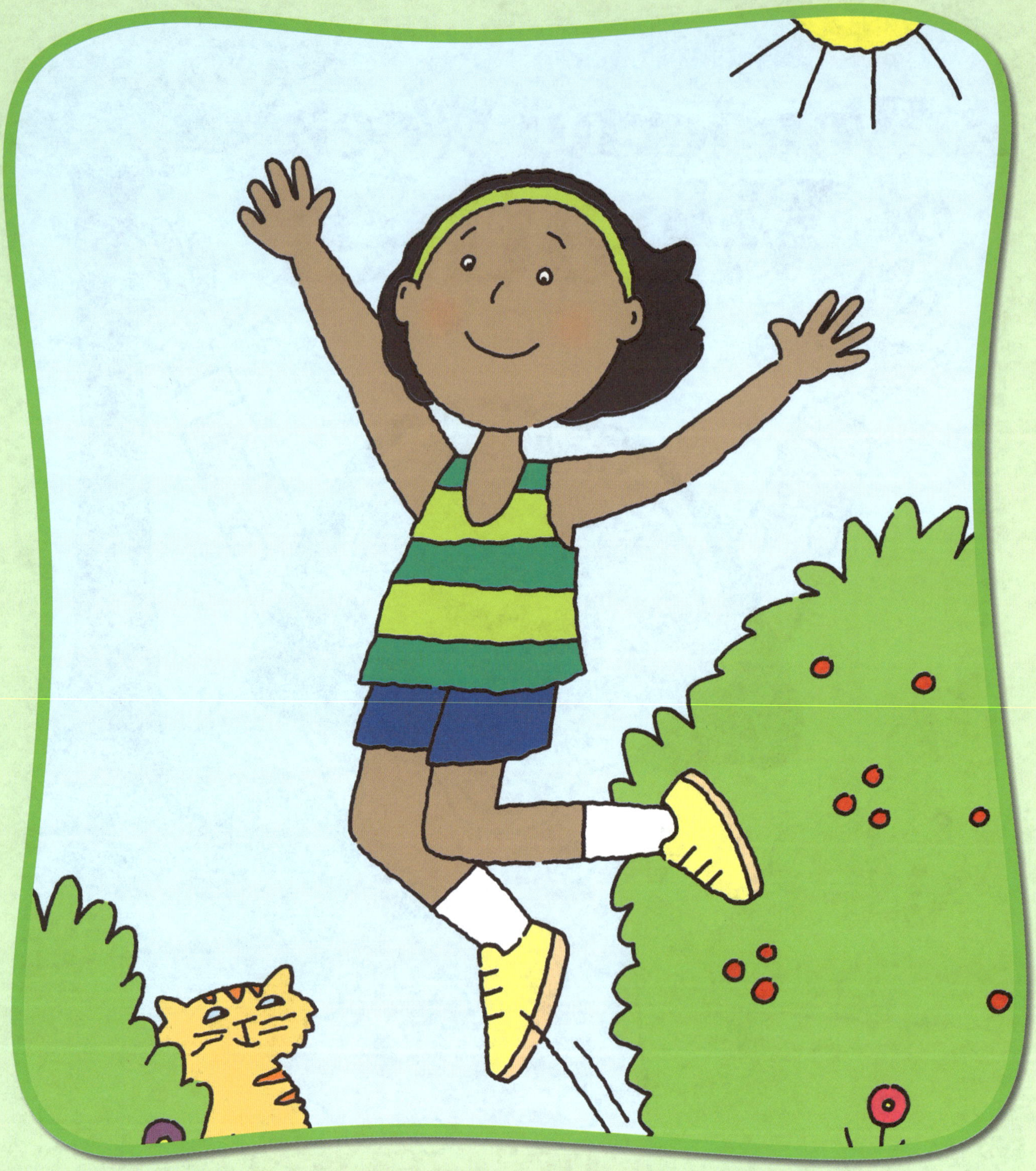

Sunday was a sunny day.
I went out to play.
I ran and jumped.

1

The sun warmed me.

Monday was a cloudy day.

I lay on my back and watched the clouds drift by. The air felt cool.

Tuesday and Wednesday
were windy days.
The wind tugged at me
and felt cold against my face.

5

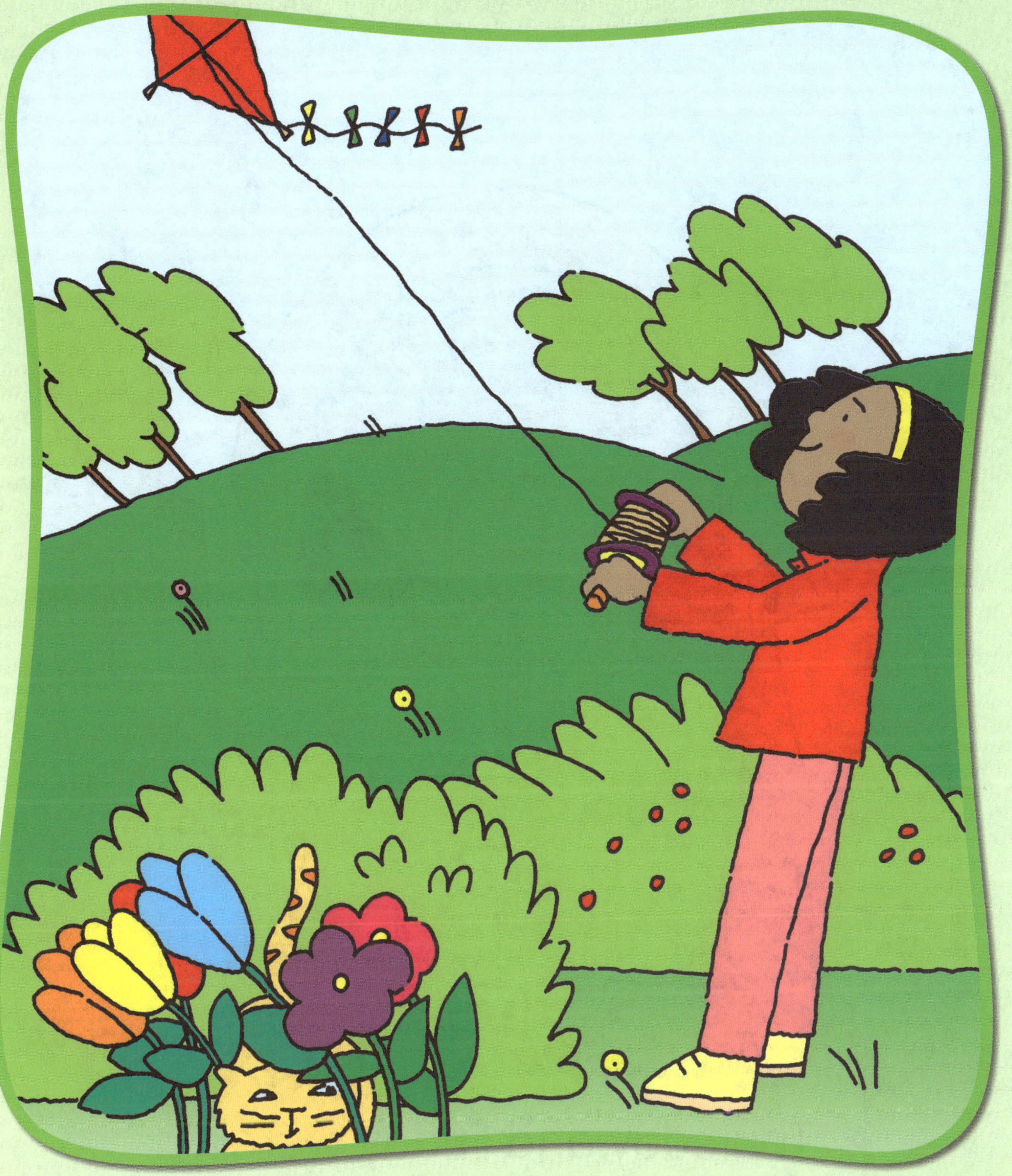

When I got home,
I flew my kite high in the sky.

6

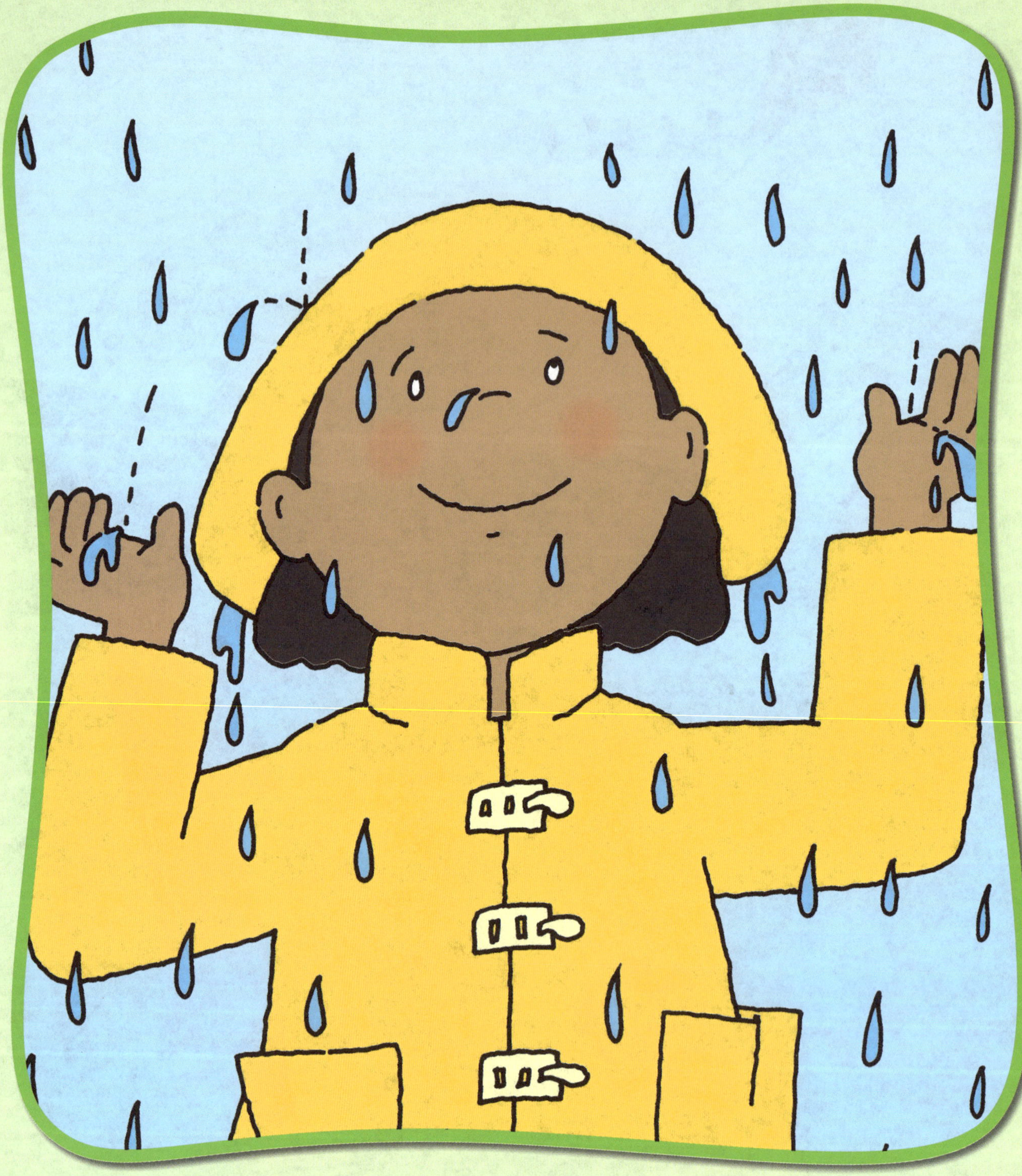

Thursday and Friday were rainy days. The rain tickled my face. It felt cold and wet.

7

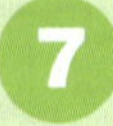

Saturday was a sunny day.
The world looked
washed and brand new.

8

The End

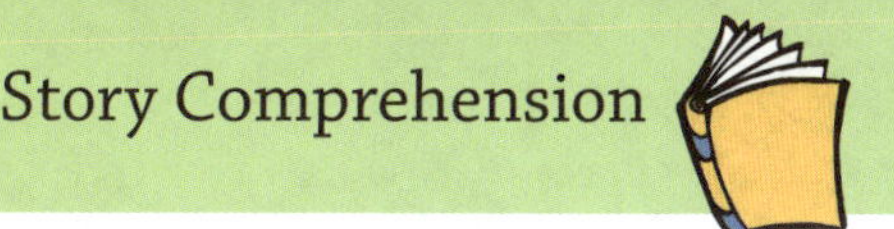

Sequence the Story

glue	glue	glue
1	2	3

Playing Outside

Color.  Cut.  Glue. 

sun	glue
rain	glue
snow	glue
wind	glue

How Many Are Left?

Count. Write.

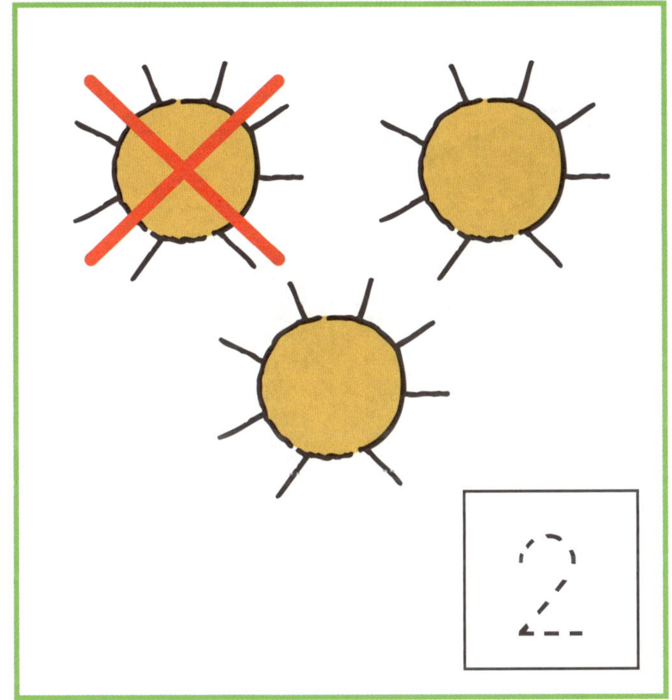

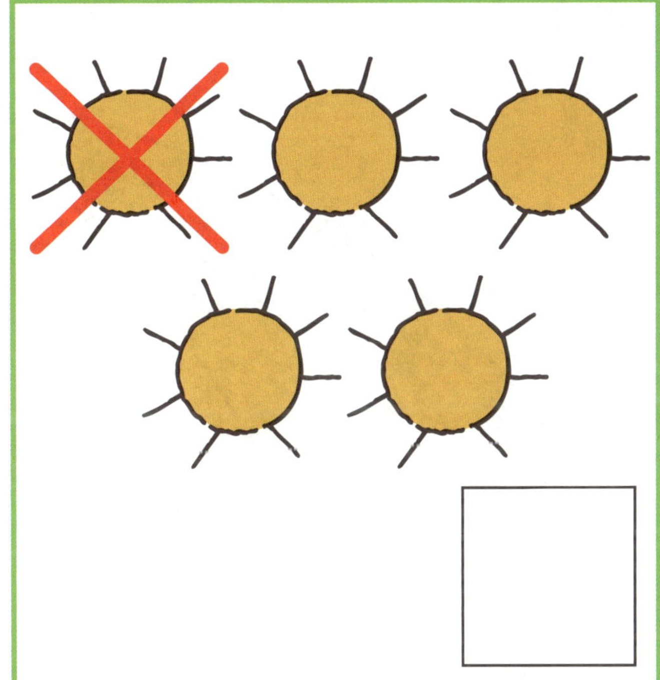

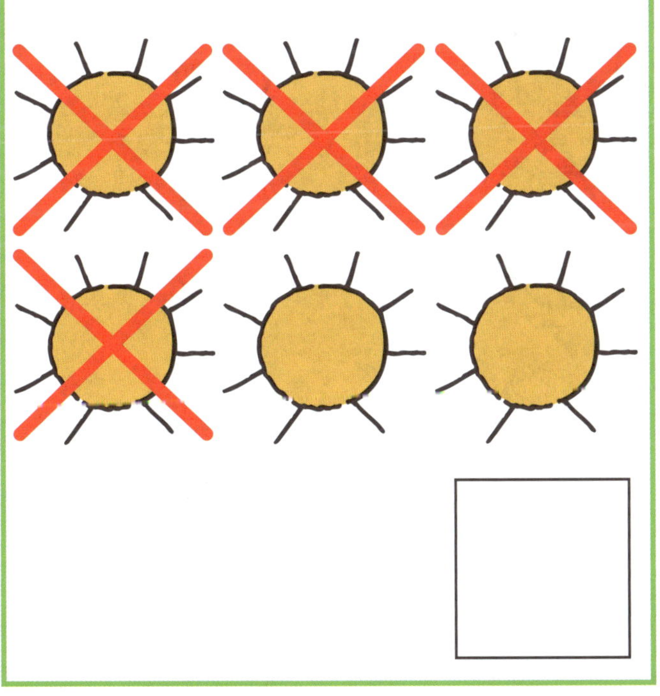

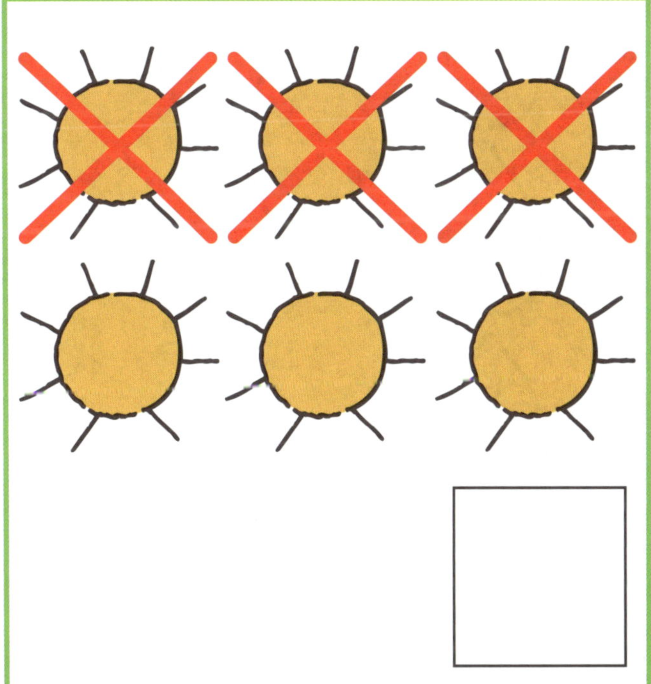

Note: Children number the raindrops from 1 through 20.

Counting Raindrops

Number the raindrops.

1 2 3 4 5 6 7 8 9 10 11 12 13 14 15 16 17 18 19 20

1

2

20

Weather
Helps Us

Look outside.
What do you see?
Wind is blowing in the tree.

Wind helps us.
It makes sailboats move.
It makes kites fly high.

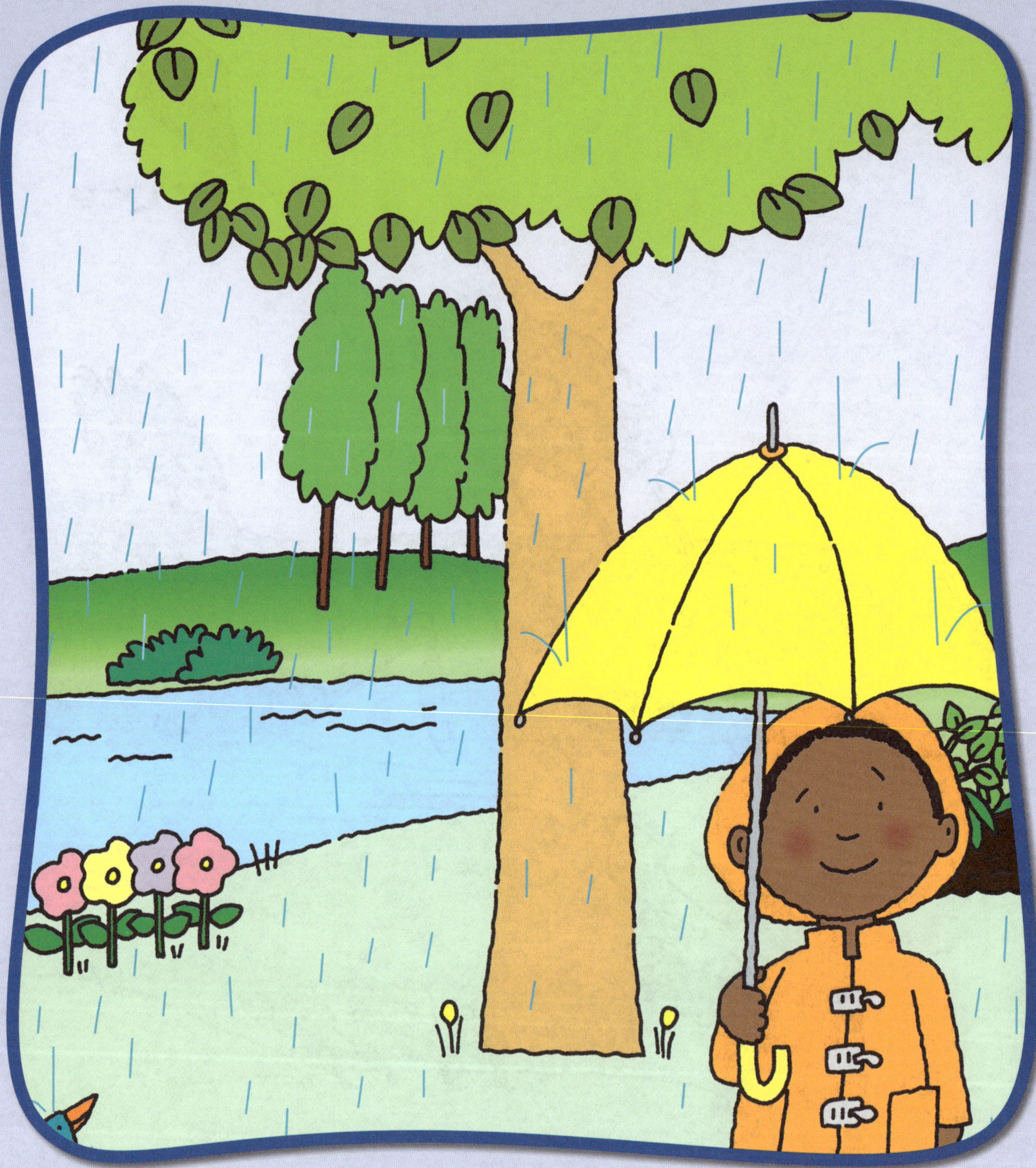

Look outside.
What do you see?
Rain is falling on the tree.

Rain helps us. Rain fills lakes and rivers with good water. Plants, animals, and people all need water to live and grow.

Look outside.
What do you see?
The sun is shining on the tree.

The sun helps us. Plants, animals, and people all need sunshine. The sun helps plants grow. People and animals eat plants.

6

Weather helps us.
I've just told you
some of the ways.

Weather helps us.
Can you tell me some of the ways?

The End

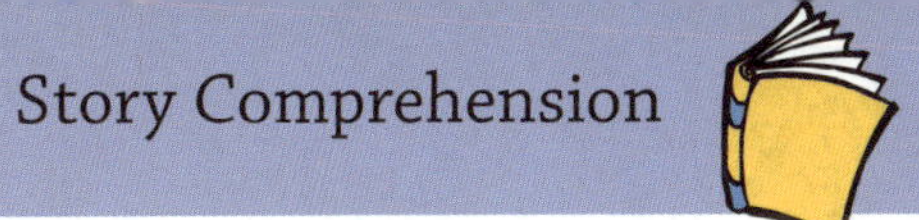

Weather Helps Us

Color. Cut. Glue.

glue	glue	glue

Which One Does Not Belong?

Mark an **X** on the picture in each row that does **not** belong.

Same Sound

Look at the first picture in each row.

Color the picture that begins with the same sound.

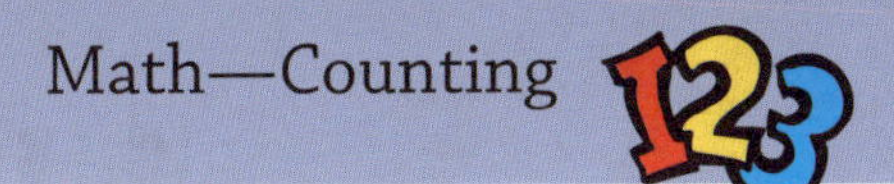

Count the Kites

Count. Write. 

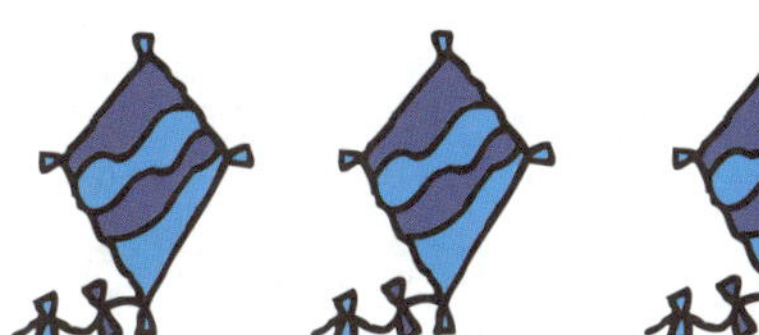

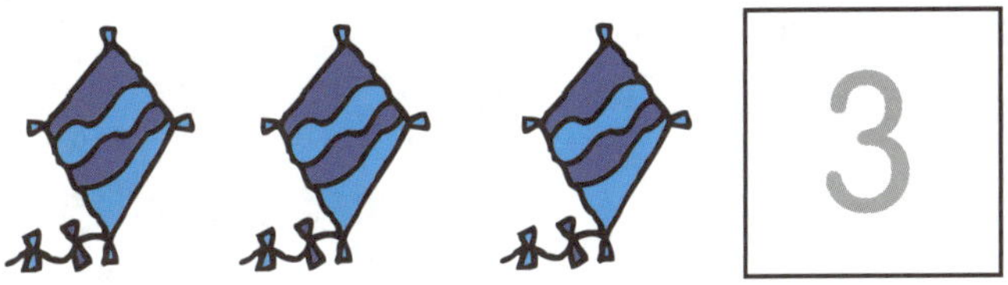

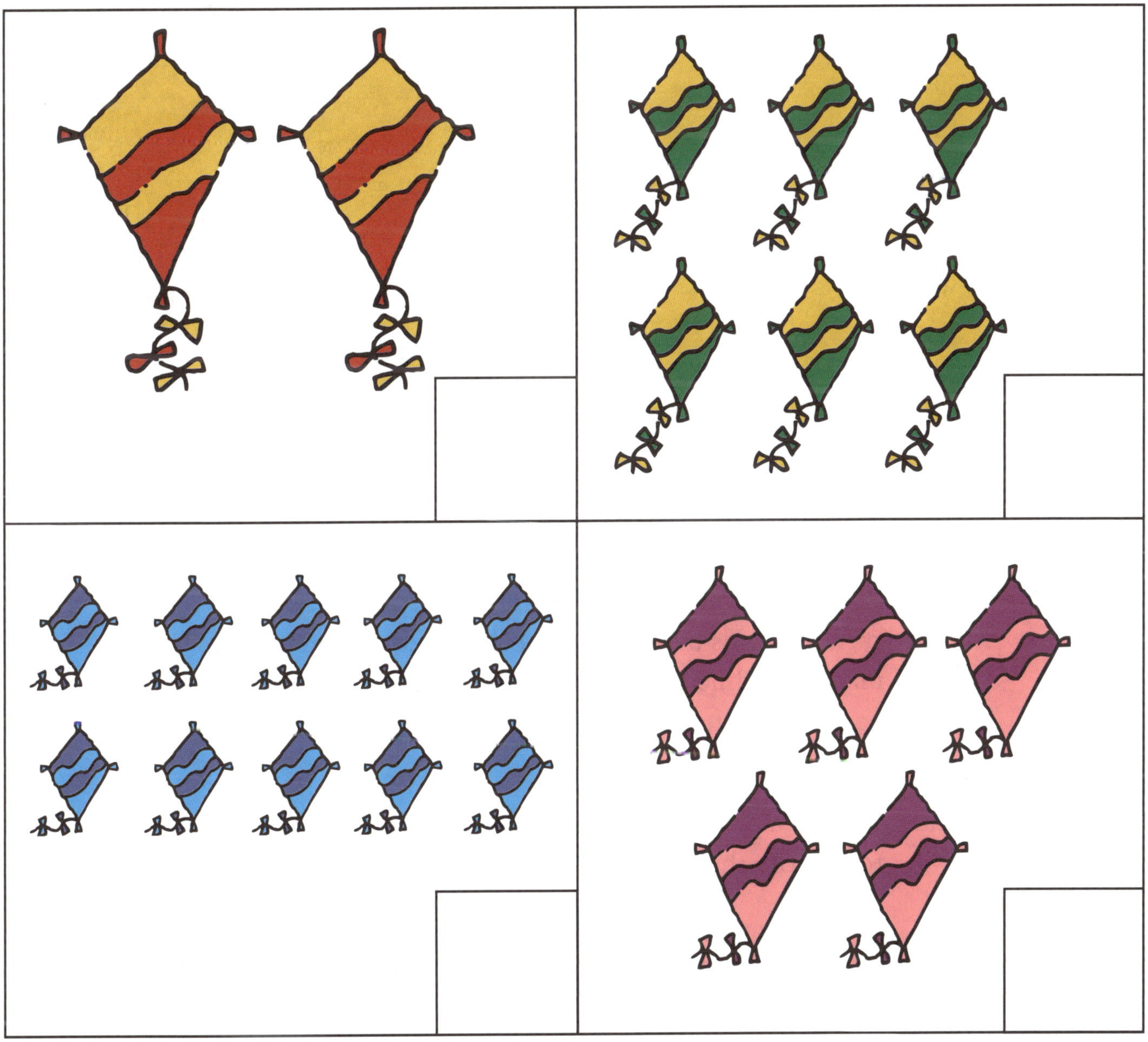

Alphabet Cards

Use these colorful alphabet cards in a variety of ways. Simply laminate and cut apart the cards and store them in a sturdy envelope or box.

Alphabet cards can be used to practice skills such as:

- letter recognition
- letter-sound association
- visual perception

Alphabet Card Games

What's My Name? Use the alphabet cards to introduce the names of the letters, both uppercase and lowercase.

Make a Match Children match a lowercase and uppercase letter. They then turn the cards over to self-check. If a correct match has been made, the child will see a picture of the same object, whose name begins with the letter being matched.

First-Sound Game Use the alphabet cards as phonics flashcards and ask children to identify the sound of each letter.

ABC Order Children take all of the uppercase or lowercase cards and place them in alphabetical order.

A	a
B	b
C	c
D	d

apple

Apple

Early Bird: Weather • EMC 7059 • © Evan-Moor Corp.

boots

Early Bird: Weather • EMC 7059 • © Evan-Moor Corp.

Boots

Early Bird: Weather • EMC 7059 • © Evan-Moor Corp.

cat

Early Bird: Weather • EMC 7059 • © Evan-Moor Corp.

Cat

Early Bird: Weather • EMC 7059 • © Evan-Moor Corp.

dig

Early Bird: Weather • EMC 7059 • © Evan-Moor Corp.

Dig

Early Bird: Weather • EMC 7059 • © Evan-Moor Corp.

E

e

F

f

G

g

H

h

egg

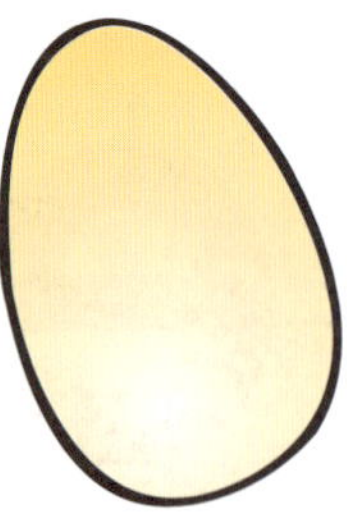

Early Bird: Weather • EMC 7059 • © Evan-Moor Corp.

Egg

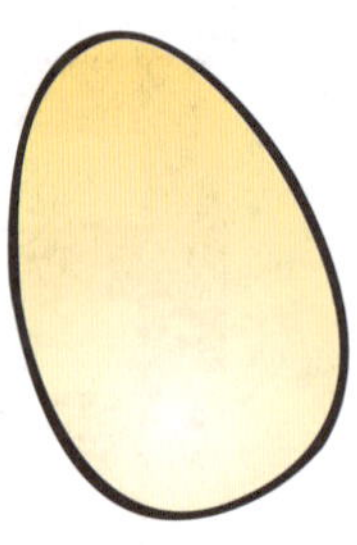

Early Bird: Weather • EMC 7059 • © Evan-Moor Corp.

face

Early Bird: Weather • EMC 7059 • © Evan-Moor Corp.

Face

Early Bird: Weather • EMC 7059 • © Evan-Moor Corp.

garden

Early Bird: Weather • EMC 7059 • © Evan-Moor Corp.

Garden

Early Bird: Weather • EMC 7059 • © Evan-Moor Corp.

hands

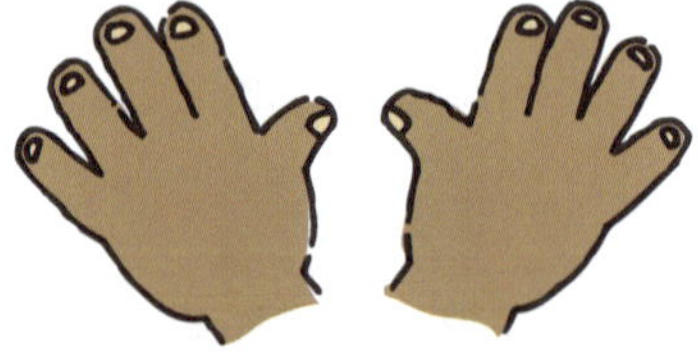

Early Bird: Weather • EMC 7059 • © Evan-Moor Corp.

Hands

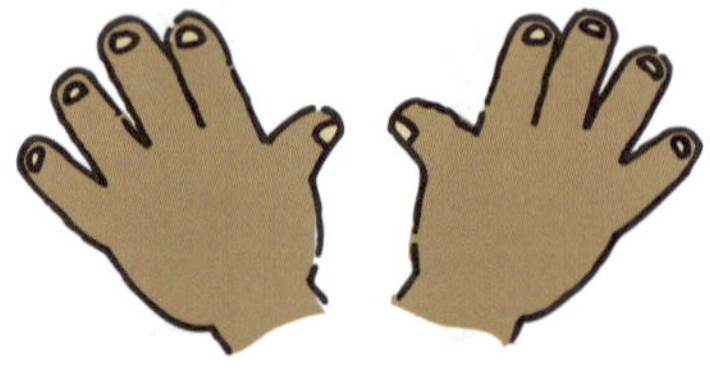

Early Bird: Weather • EMC 7059 • © Evan-Moor Corp.

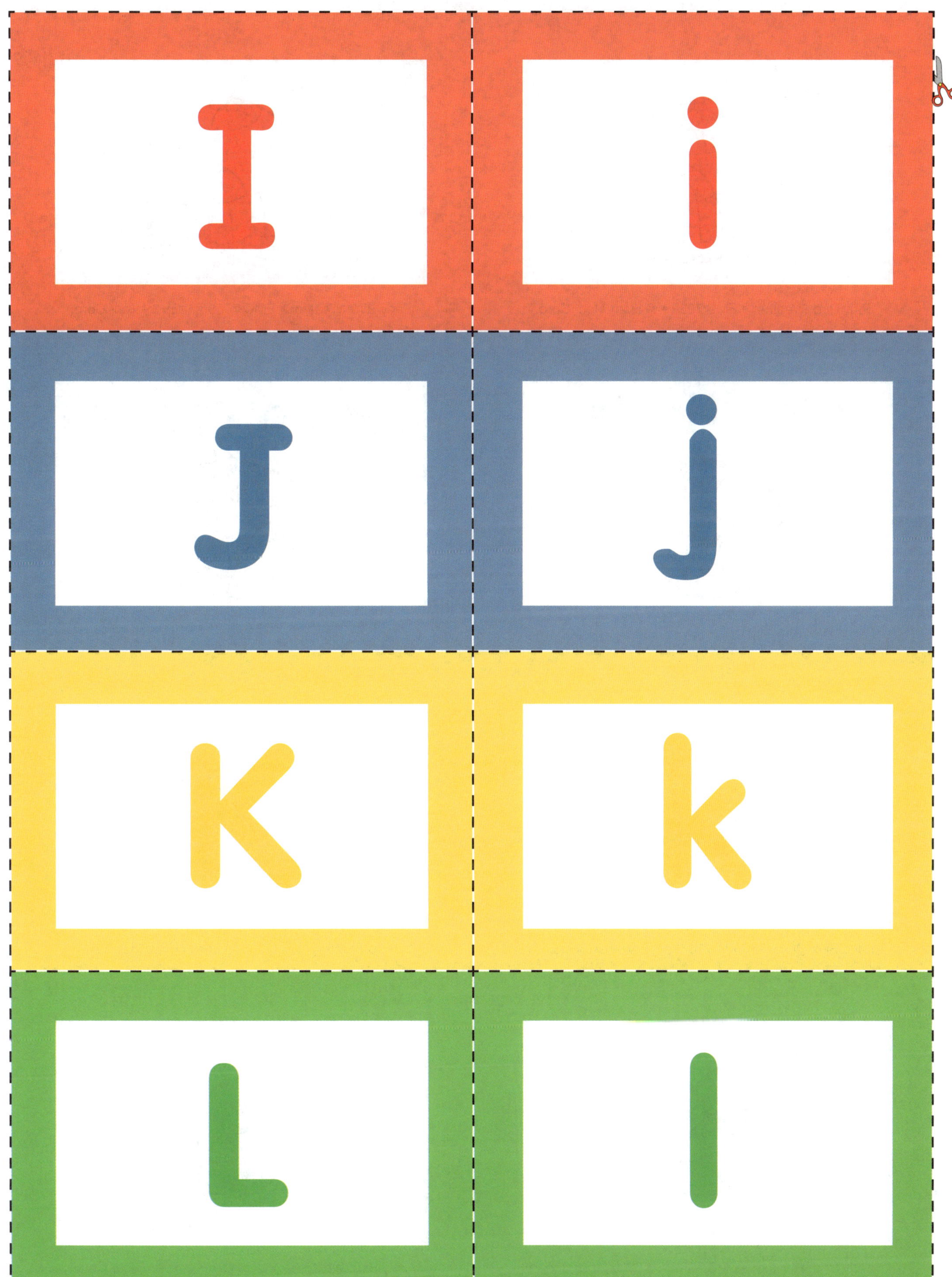
I
i
J
j
K
k
L
l

igloo

Early Bird: Weather • EMC 7059 • © Evan-Moor Corp.

Igloo

Early Bird: Weather • EMC 7059 • © Evan-Moor Corp.

jack-o'-lantern

Early Bird: Weather • EMC 7059 • © Evan-Moor Corp.

Jack-o'-lantern

Early Bird: Weather • EMC 7059 • © Evan-Moor Corp.

kite

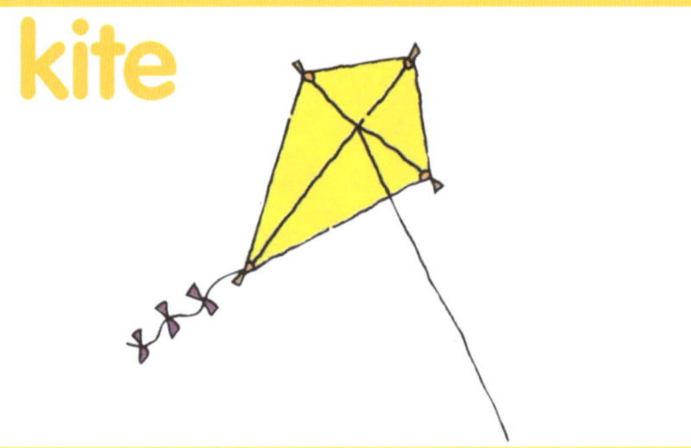

Early Bird: Weather • EMC 7059 • © Evan-Moor Corp.

Kite

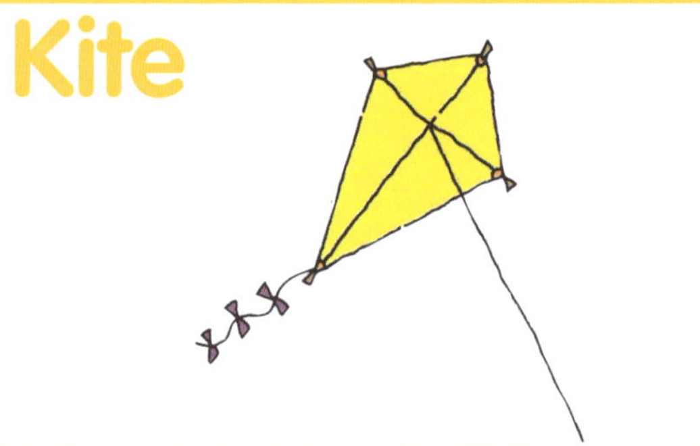

Early Bird: Weather • EMC 7059 • © Evan-Moor Corp.

leaf

Early Bird: Weather • EMC 7059 • © Evan-Moor Corp.

Leaf

Early Bird: Weather • EMC 7059 • © Evan-Moor Corp.

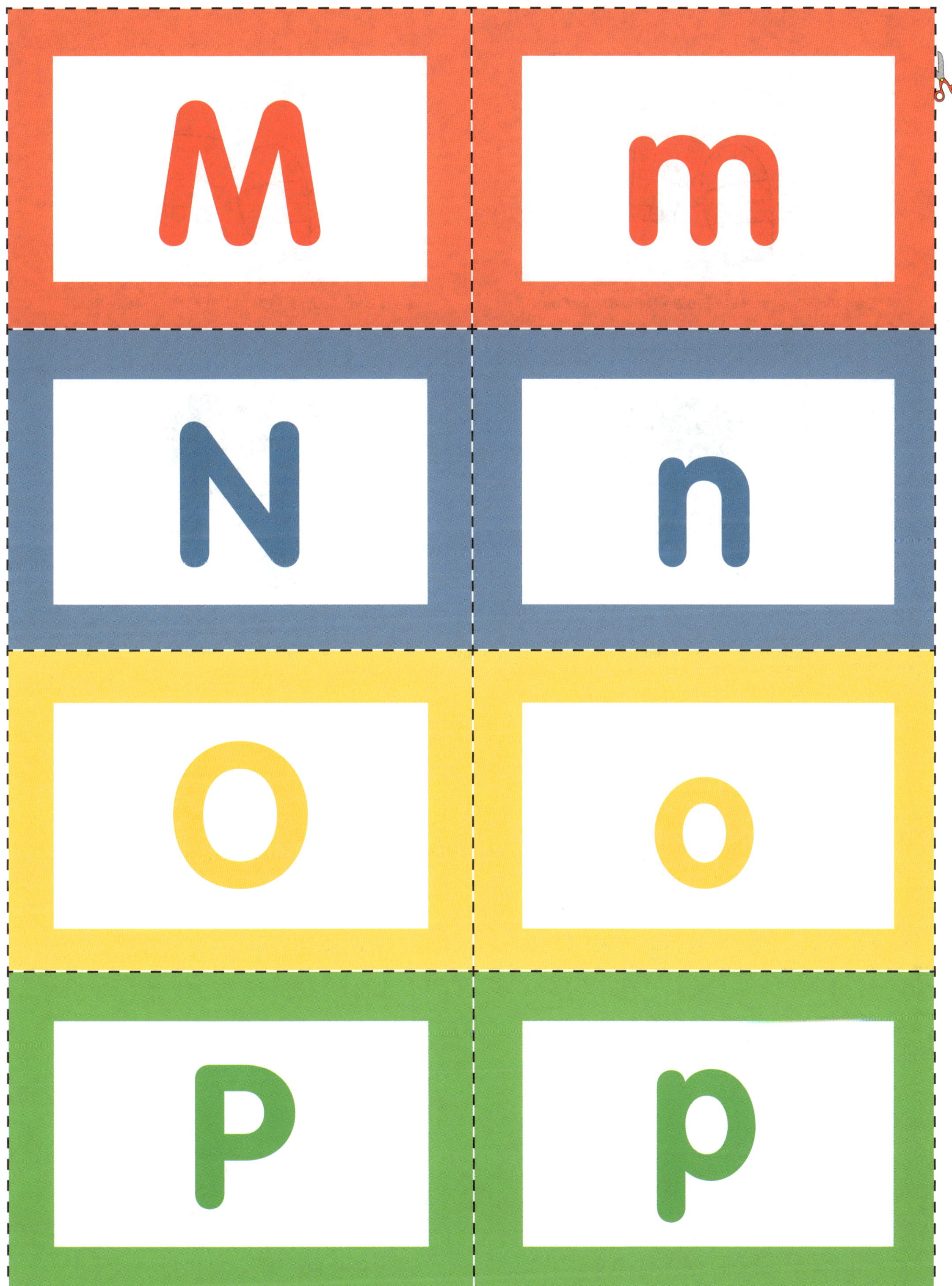
M
m
N
n
O
o
P
p

mittens

Mittens

Early Bird: Weather • EMC 7059 • © Evan-Moor Corp.

nest

Early Bird: Weather • EMC 7059 • © Evan-Moor Corp.

Nest

Early Bird: Weather • EMC 7059 • © Evan-Moor Corp.

Early Bird: Weather • EMC 7059 • © Evan-Moor Corp.

On/Off

Early Bird: Weather • EMC 7059 • © Evan-Moor Corp.

puddle

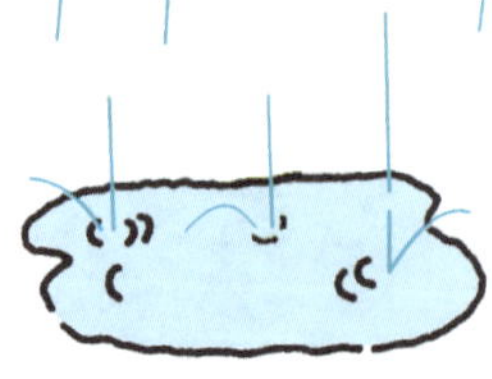

Early Bird: Weather • EMC 7059 • © Evan-Moor Corp.

Puddle

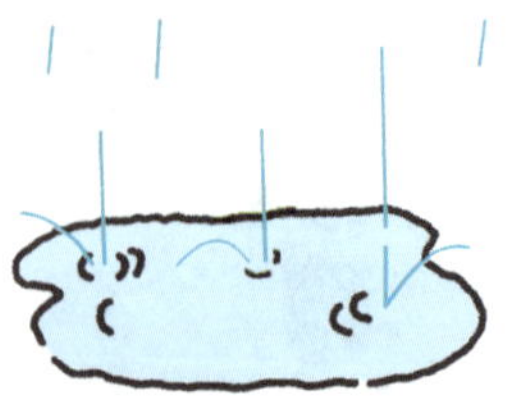

Early Bird: Weather • EMC 7059 • © Evan-Moor Corp.

Q
q
R
r
S
s
T
t

quickly

Quickly

Early Bird: Weather • EMC 7059 • © Evan-Moor Corp.

rain

Early Bird: Weather • EMC 7059 • © Evan-Moor Corp.

Rain

Early Bird: Weather • EMC 7059 • © Evan-Moor Corp.

sun

Early Bird: Weather • EMC 7059 • © Evan-Moor Corp.

Sun

Early Bird: Weather • EMC 7059 • © Evan-Moor Corp.

tank top

Early Bird: Weather • EMC 7059 • © Evan-Moor Corp.

Tank top

Early Bird: Weather • EMC 7059 • © Evan-Moor Corp.

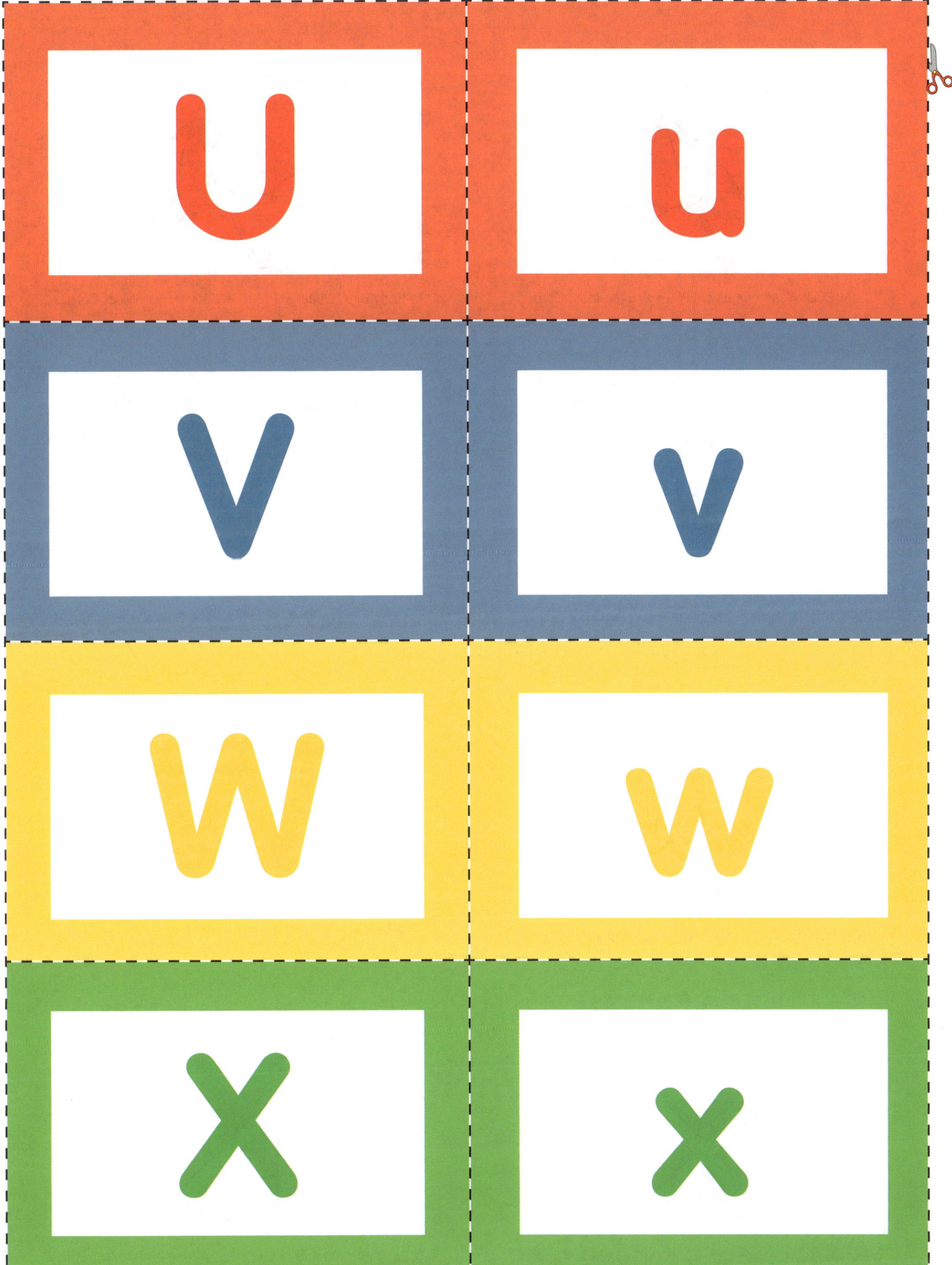
U
u
V
v
W
w
X
x

umbrella

Umbrella

Early Bird: Weather • EMC 7059 • © Evan-Moor Corp.

vines

Early Bird: Weather • EMC 7059 • © Evan-Moor Corp.

Vines

Early Bird: Weather • EMC 7059 • © Evan-Moor Corp.

wind

Early Bird: Weather • EMC 7059 • © Evan-Moor Corp.

Wind

Early Bird: Weather • EMC 7059 • © Evan-Moor Corp.

x on a gate

Early Bird: Weather • EMC 7059 • © Evan-Moor Corp.

X on a gate

Early Bird: Weather • EMC 7059 • © Evan-Moor Corp.

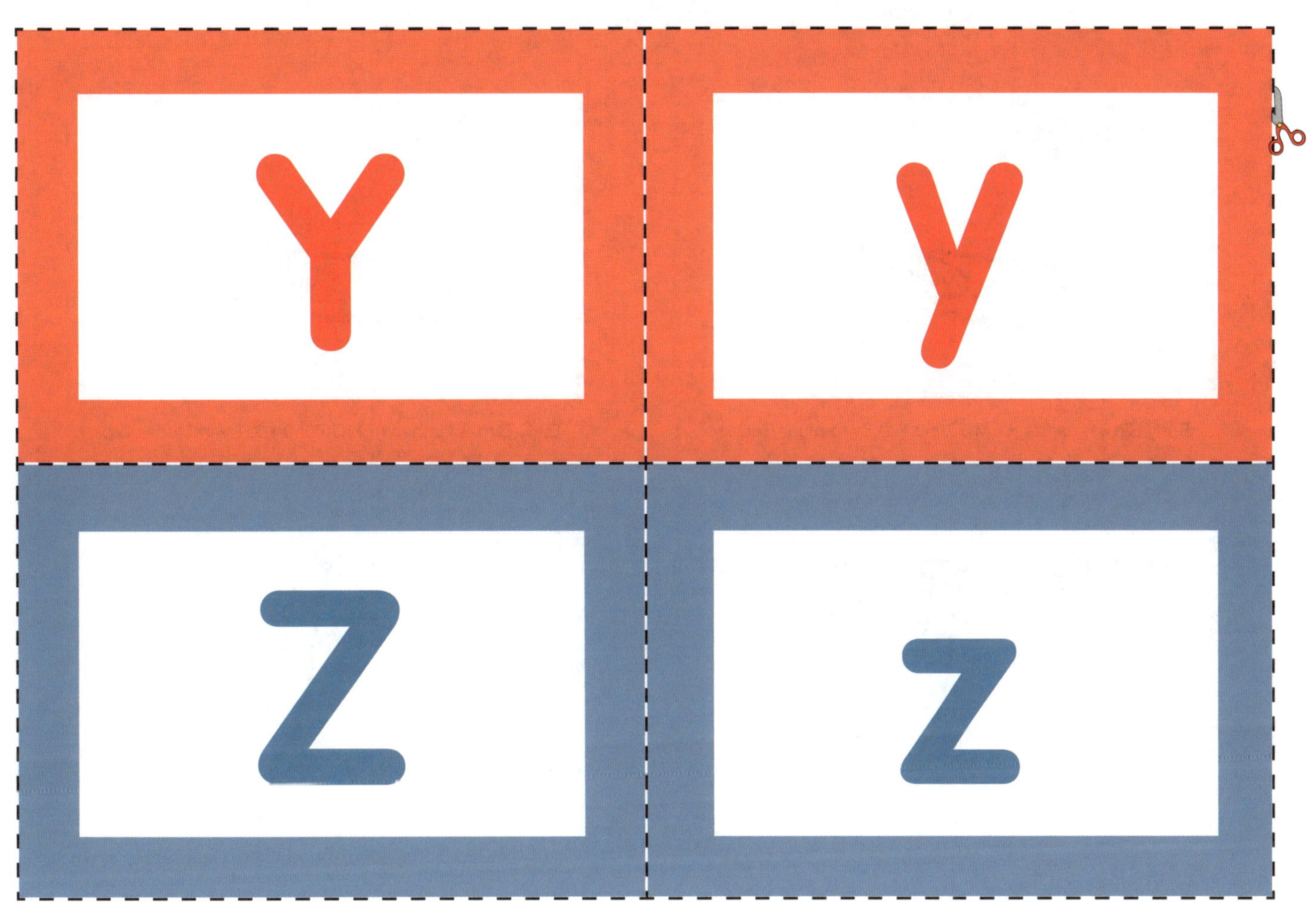
Y
y
Z
z

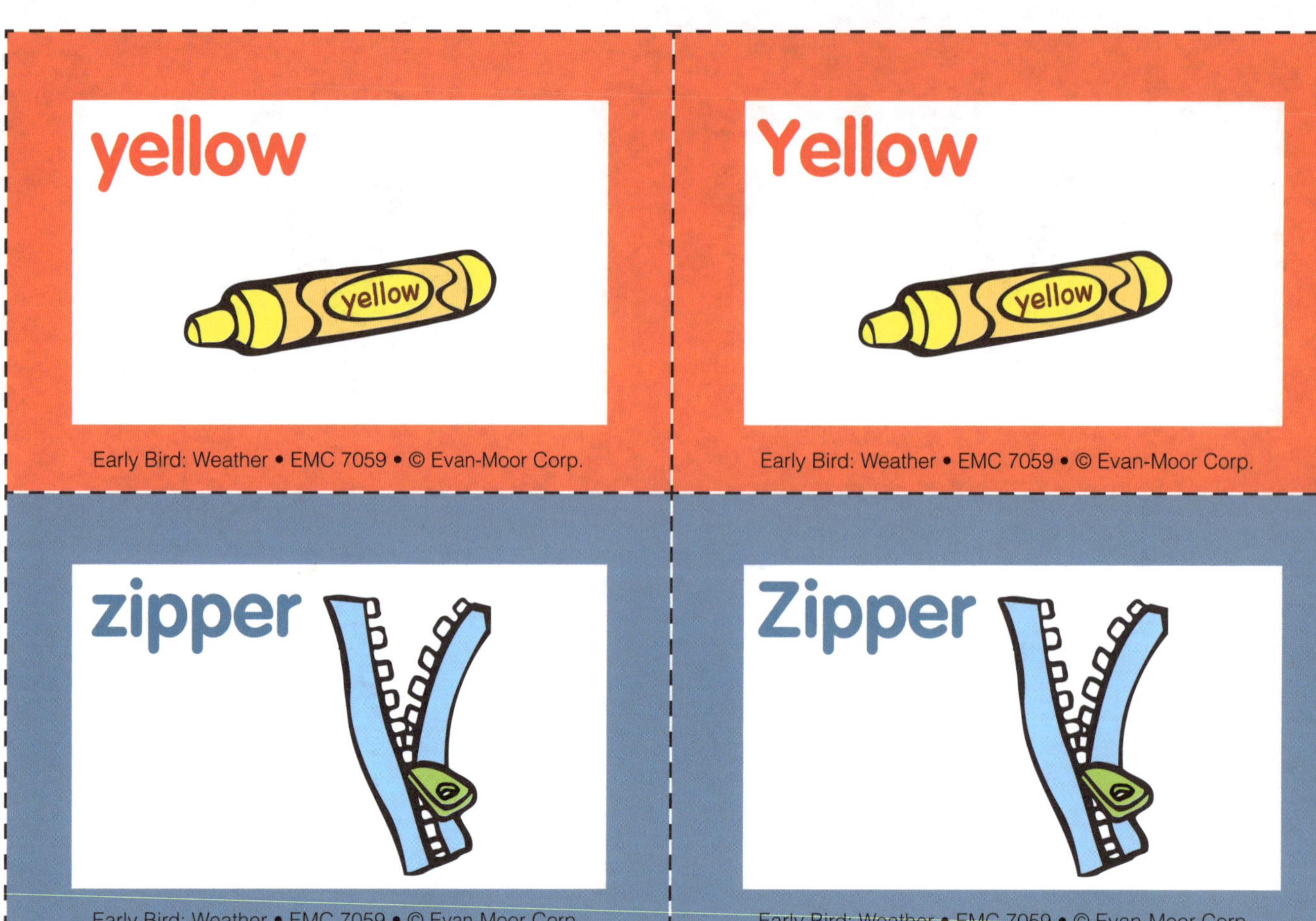
yellow
yellow
Early Bird: Weather • EMC 7059 • © Evan-Moor Corp.
Yellow
yellow
Early Bird: Weather • EMC 7059 • © Evan-Moor Corp.
zipper
Early Bird: Weather • EMC 7059 • © Evan-Moor Corp.
Zipper
Early Bird: Weather • EMC 7059 • © Evan-Moor Corp.

Answer Key

Page 13

Page 14

Page 15

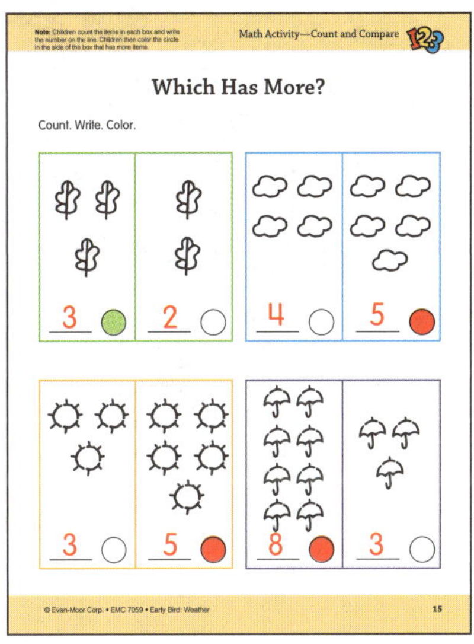

Page 16

Page 27

Page 29

Page 31

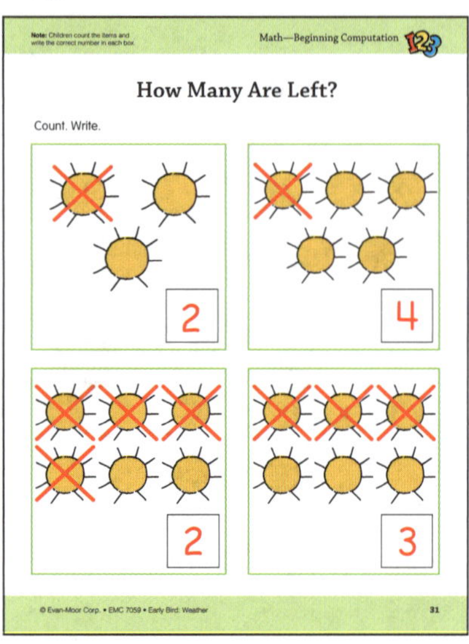

Page 32

Page 43

Page 45

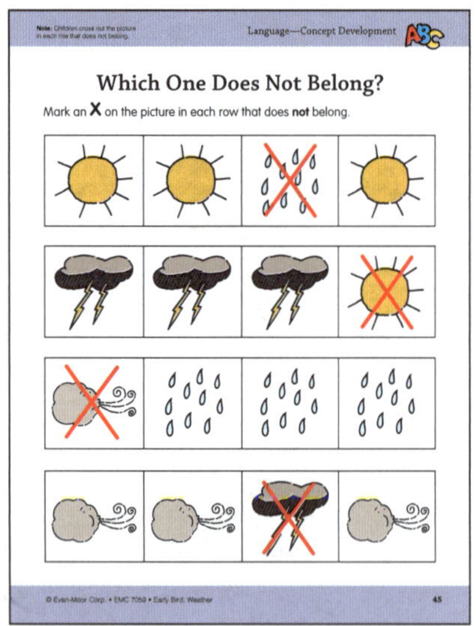

Page 46

Page 47

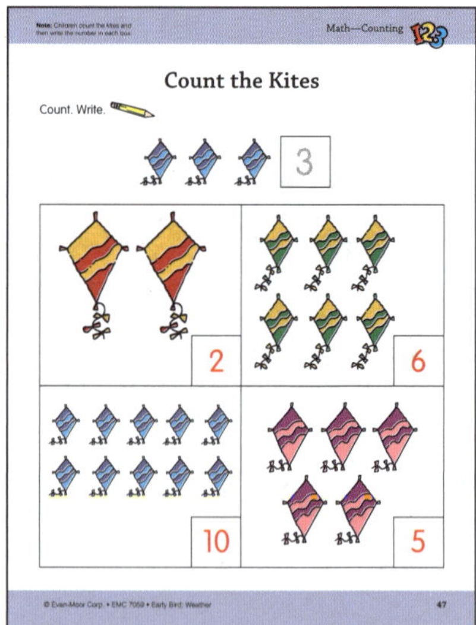